PRAISE FOR

Ever wonder what would have happened if Kathy Acker and Flannery O'Connor had collaborated on a book of poems? The result may have looked something (although nowhere close) to Jessie Janeshek's latest book... *Spanish Donkey/Pear of Anguish* is pure punch-poetry, it never misses a beat and it certainly never misses its mark. Read this book and be changed. Or better yet, read this book and change.
    —James Diaz, *Anti-Heroin Chic*

The poems deliver verses on seductive female stars from the films of the 1930s and beyond. Like the stars they're watching, the poems become the empowered ones: language is theirs to play with, to betray....Each poem is impeccably crafted, syllable by syllable. The line breaks are as good as a crisp Pinot Grigio. No, wait, for the Bette and Lucy poems, pour yourself a martini. The Perpignan poems might like a tumbler of rosé."
    —from the preface to *Invisible Mink* by Marilyn Kallet

This is what Janeshek does at her best—interweaves everyday life, the glamour and tragedy of old Hollywood, and our innermost fears and neuroses, which she bravely points out in herself so that we can identify.
    —Shaindel Beers, *Contrary Magazine*

Invisible Mink is a book of empowerment. Syntactically risky and rigorous, Janeshek's narrators orbit around women—actresses of the great black-and-whites (indeed, Bette Davis makes the first appearance)—but also fictional characters of literary import such as Lucy Snowe, the protagonist of Charlotte Brontë's 1853 novel, *Villette*, who recurs several times within the book... *Invisible Mink* empowers—not only its author and the females on which it centers—but its readers, as well, as they come away with its energy refreshed and privy to a truly original voice.
    —William Wright, *Town Creek Poetry*

MADCAP

ALSO BY JESSIE JANESHEK

JESSIE
JANESHEK
MADCAP

STALKING HORSE PRESS
SANTA FE, NEW MEXICO

MADCAP

Copyright © 2019 By Jessie Janeshek
ISBN: 978-0-9991152-9-9
Library Of Congress Data Available on Request

First paperback edition published by Stalking Horse Press, October 2019

www.stalkinghorsepress.com

Design by James Reich

Stalking Horse Press
Santa Fe, New Mexico

"Tragedy is a close-up, comedy a long shot."

—*Buster Keaton*

CONTENTS

THE CLOSE-UP

THE LONG SHOT

THE CLOSE-UP

MADCAP / TOUCH UP

it's all lies and bumps and you can see lumps
and I used to hate talking   but pills make it better
        I'm not always reflecting in red.
I stopped painting my nails because I couldn't stand
                the lack of perfection
to lie without a topcoat   so much frankincense
        and am I being tacky?   It helps to go out
                but I should be grateful for the candle crown
                        sweet buns, extra light.

A dream is a wish you synthpop
        and were I in Amsterdam I'd wear fake braids
I'd pray for cameras every day
        avoidance behavior   one tacky dress
            as a dark woman knocked   at each door and window.

        I try to touch up my manicure
a week since the man etched *you'll die*   in the mud
                but I'm still alive so I'm super confused.

                                    beautiful image
♡ I wake up every day a corpse flower at my most terrible
            chipped nails and a shot in the arm
            I put money where your mouth is
or I hide the money   in your underwear
            or since all crooners are sad   in your velvet poinsettias

Harlow is rolling   her past in a rug
and selling her assets
        or Harlow is rotting
making too many films with titles like *Bombshell*
        knowing our futures will get us in noir
no matter how long our eyelashes are.

YOU NEVER GO BACK
ONCE YOU'RE A BLONDE

the hottub   the absence
      the more thunder coming   the life of the mind
but what if the last sister lingered
      a crime inchoate   a bathroom filled
                        with her blood and pink light
and what if the last sister lingered
      to say you need meaning   you need a routine
      and what if you think   you're not good enough
                        for a dress or a drug or a dream
      and you don't trust your mind
            and it's self-sabotage   in heart-shaped sunglasses
      and needles in the scene
      and side hustle/slit wrist   breaking your row of perfumes
on the vanity tray.   You wear a red sailor blouse
      tight waist   walk through the woods smoking
or you see little changes   watching the dailies
      as the month drains away
or you lie and say   you're washing the windows
or you lie and say   sweat and sunset
                  do not trust these clouds
                  and a blonde can stop time
or a blonde joke can stop   the light in your side
      but he says your idiosyncrasy
is how the law of the underworld stings
      a semen-filled condom   left at the scene
he says it's common   and you'll always be funny

and all the young women are guilty of something
and just wait for him to say what.

PUT YOUR MONEY IN YOUR MOUTH AND ASK WHEN YOU'LL MARRY AND HAVE A HAPPY HOME AND NOT A HAPPY HOUR

It's the thinner the faux fur   you've had since 13
          the Sabbath a promise of rest
but really the promise of death.
          Some say California   is so bleak on Christmas
                    but I know it's orange glitter
          of course I only know   one way out of here
oblivious to Coney Island   and the witching waves
                    saving cash in a cage.
I eat without thinking   thick cream, a black bathing suit
          but once I was comfortable
now too many lights   no streets safe to walk on
          sticky lip lacquer   and crying so hard
                    I can't drive or dance.

We turn the heat up
          turn the heat down   smoke and fuck without thinking.
                    It's the thinner your coat in the mist
          it's the power flickering.
I sit on the soldier ghost's lap   over and over
          walk past the Alamo broke.
          Everything here is mud red and I'm lonely
the man in spats doesn't invite me   to his gangster movie
          but how sweet to indulge in cheap beer and faint
like Lana Turner   or forage for food on Bullsboro.

                In the utopia there are no footprints
the deer in the mirror   and the glass hooves
        keep acting the snow   queen in the rain
and I laugh at the thought that this is my bedroom
        a velvet settee   and no bloodstains.

HOW TO EQUATE   MADCAP WITH DARKNESS

First there was the death hoax
and then the real death   and I banked my rehab
     hair broken and thin   since girls don't need love
     just personality
staid divination   on the flood plain
     the spirit of the house
     an acrylic base   a tortoiseshell sheen in the rain
     there's a lot to be dead about
♡   and I can't or won't pray.

I arrive at Cry Wolf   with soft victory rolls
     chilly and cinnamon   houndstooth and white cloak
I wake up and sink   and there's not so much left of me
     to let go my biography   gun shoved at my silk
the glittery waste   black bows on the wrists
     and the crazy equestrian   jumps out the window
     smashing my mother's antique jar of cold cream

     and maybe work in the way   you crush up the drugs
lacing pills as I sneak   in the dumbwaiter
     disorientation   lifting myself to your lab
     and I crawl across rooftops in rain
     and I like my look
     burning the books as I grow out a pixie cut
     occult and hunger
     and you like the weather

sticky baby fingerprints and transitional sequence
            and you said tragedy   brought us together
        as the servant cleaned up after the body
            and I needed a lesson in intricacy or intensity
beetle brooches and other bad luck jewelry
                how a river makes a town
            runs it with so many doubts
                a bed only for sex or for sleep.

MADCAP IN THE DARK

I hate myself and my pain
close the blinds so they can't see   my silver tree
         looking good enough in the vapors
to be a foggy Lana Turner profane angel singing carols
         or blood-lipped in the manger scene
or wrapped in plaid with laryngitis   to kill men with good makeup
         and I don't mean to make you sad
but when we came back you had draped the tree with grapes
         and smeared the lens with Vaseline.

Haunted dolls   a holiday   ask harder leave your kidneys
         haunted daddy finger waves
                  I don't want to fuck   and I'll wear velvet lounge pant
your hounds dragging me   and we might get shot
         as we sweat on New Year's Eve.

Bow wire in the pines   and I'm touching up my manicure
         trying to smooth things over
this is sadness jangling
         my Christmas past veins in the trees
this is you couldn't care less for your body
         your Christmas past envelope too dark for ink
a diet of hotdogs   and Coney Island powder puffs
         skulls and 8-balls and god bless the hogs

god bless the red machine guessing your weight
        this is you couldn't care less for your soul
will I cry for the vapors/cry for the veins
       the trashheap cats come
             toward my scotch for warmth.

MADCAP / MARI LWYD

You'll get in trouble   you keep speaking your mind
    stuck in this house   stuck in the dark
relief gets no sign.
    I don't want to turn to the bottle but how can I not
        I can't hardly stand
silver trees and the faux leopard coats
    full moons and corpse hunts under the meteor
showers mean nothing.   We colorize   we codify
    domestic scenes so they're cozy.

I won't be happy until I embarrass
        hide the baubles away   until I saturate
    and Christmas lights burn for two days straight
after a murder.   His heart on the branch
    and me licking the spoon   in the tinny play kitchen.

What was time like   what a haunt/what a hole
    stuck in the horse costume
madcap, it's a lie   as my body tries to adjust
      to the clean hair game   and the wasted foreboding
      and the lack of trust
sadness lighting the wicks of all dead candles
    in my candle crown   and you'll smell like fish
                if you let us burn
    all the clothes in your kitchen.

I try to focus   write down older numbers
       I try to take   my drugs and just go
             I ask was it because of the vampires
No? You think you're getting your way
             all you're doing is chasing the ghosts
       behind the wood panels.
I was going to be modern and honest
       I was going to stop being noir scum
but I'm drowning in wax and your demons won't leave me alone.

but, I'm constantly drowning in My own demons.
       Rewritten

HOUSE OF WAX / GOOD SCOTCH FOR PAIN

open it back up   trounce the romance
I can't take this darkness   snow but no ice cream
          milkmaid-tight braids.
The cat ran away   Lombard was an absurdist
          however there is no emergency
leaning over the crystal ball   beautifully lit
          no lesbian scenes cut.

                              Lombard was a child once
and there was that time I was made to lose the spelling bee
          slipped in my black and blue checkered dress
cracked my head off the locker   and it was a rumor how to spell st
          how to deal with the villain
at the slumber party dressed like a showgirl
          how to deal with the villain   when you could not show your tit

          I told the girls I was in the sleeping bag
with Charlie but there was no emergency
          the cat's ears soft and pink over the coals
the taxidermist saved   800 chickens
          and winter's the season   for taxidermy
blue hair and traitors   pink throats and pull it together
                    and it's in bad taste
                    and it's in bad therapy
          and I dream my nails drip
and I dream I string the big deer
          and you're all terrible
and I dream I want you to die

and sometimes I give up   communing with darkness
   and this works best if you don't
  believe my experiment
    except when we drink.

ARBOREAL HOUSE WAX /
DID ME LIKE THAT

Snow on the devil and my ghost fell over
    then again this was alone time
then again I'd never tire
    of the red town church square every night
  loose meat in the tornado shelter
    masked boys riding by
      in the cold-chromey cars
    screaming *don't break the goats!*
then again opals and crushing up pills
    wood, chains, and light
      ok, that's pretty good
    a coat closet, morphine, and tits in the dollhouse
      badness and blackness and my jewel-toned nightie.
I'm afraid of the night. I'm afraid of soap operas
  on the Predicta TV. I'm afraid of leaving something
      at the injection site.
I'm afraid of the wood   smoking near triple wicks
    playing twins in a split screen
red wig, I'm in Brooklyn
    when I wear the gold heels
      I fuck like a dog
    pyramidal points cutting straight from the wood.

Yes, this was alone time   and you only said
        something nice about me
since I said something nice about you
          art-deco lanterns   antecedent anniversaries
            a lime-green smock dress
            shaking like Saturn
vodka straight from the bottle
          you're laying an egg   in your foreign bed
            is it your back   or is it your kidneys?
I'm lying blue-cold in the orchard
          but I've horsed around
and isn't it lucky in the movie
          you two are in love
          and I end up hanging myself
          or I keep swinging   bon-bons past the flames
            isn't it lucky as I lie in the twine spiderweb
          my hair curls like Veronica Lake?

          All these new women
        keep coming up in bad faith
            and the pressure of welcoming someone
and I touch the doorframe obsessive/compulsive
            and I touch a little
of your confession   but it's limp fatalism
            and now my third eye is so tired.

HOUSE OF WAX / FREE O'FROST

You ask why I'm still chopping
pumpkin on a stick   hens and chicks
       when it's not worth it   give yourself apoplexy
heat's on/a top knot   we walk through pseudo-winter
              you say I'll regret complaining
       when all men stop whistling
       you say you can't stop crying
              about prairie city
his skin falling off his skull in the yard.

I was drunk in a past life
       I always kept a noose in the room
desolate, spicy, and wild just in case.
       Now I go out to piss
              behind spooky pines
       since it makes me feel like an animal.
                     I go out in my vinyl
              Halloween costume
                     and plastic mask
       I keep lapping up blood to feel full
              I don't wear gloves
              and I owe myself
                     the longest apology.

The glittery deer   wears the longest
            eyelashes 'til me.
I eat eight pieces of pizza
        sew my lashes on   once I numb myself
            with booze and cocaine.
You say old money/new money   stratified sadness
        Hollywood forever   erroneous gold jacquard robes.
            You say unwrap the deer   get out of my house
        but I was drunk in a past life
            crash-crushy velvet.

                    High winds, no forgiveness
                    the man spanked me over and over
                        no gloves
                    a beastling has-been
                    hot roots on the lit
                        route to stardom
                    illegal schemes and my scar
                        bloated like your inflatable

(Noun)
Dead body   ♡   corpse in pink lipstick
lifeless vessel
human•   weak star but there's still room for me
                    in the dark snow of late-nite TV.

HOUSE OF WAX / HUNT SEAT

The pink fades pretty quickly   in a general sense
    light-haired girls looking good
in soft, icy colors   on their dead green skin
    stitched up like November.
I give myself no time   and I curse the time
    in the grey bathtub   hot sausage and dogskin
Nebraska northward   boxcutter/boxelder
    and necrotic signs.   I slip up   smear my cum
    on the wall of the living room
 set up the Predicta   TV hissing a flame
    leave the garbage to rot   in the kitchen with peaches and crème.

You make a nest of my deaths and my chrome
    my mushroom necklaces, dreams
forget I was excited once.
    I wore skeleton gloves and danced like a swan
        and you curse my interests
    my weird accoutrements   times I tried to shine
dead days and dry hair and heaves
    and me falling asleep in the wood-paneled room
in the grey vacancy
        as The Chordettes moaned Mr. Sandman
    and of course that one bitch
      likes the clocks turning back
little steps here and there   tied up in the cold.

It's bad therapy
or I just stopped caring   *be orchid/be cozy*
and sometimes I bundle   vow to rise early
past any distraction
and leave for the campfire
and go ahead, run me over
my soap operas went off the air.
And sometimes I bundle   after a lover
hope I don't drip
hope I don't chip off
lilac fingernail polish   ♡
touching inside me.

HOUSE OF WAX 2

Staring into the pot like Dracula's daughter
     the pool in October   transitions erased
my head is jealous   encasing your youth and your tutu
     no air in here   but I'm asking for it.

I wish I could be you   but the disappearing carrot stew
     is how I see myself
or the crème candelabra   compulsively buying
     elemental lipstick   blue undertone shimmer.

The girl in the house arrest anklet
     says the old couple made their asylum matte red
     pissing and shitting   mole crickets in bed
     candleflames snapping   hidden lexicons
     pulling the tubes out   joinery sad and bad
     hearing the cows moo at sundown
chokecherry beat/bleat   his skin hangs like a mask.

They made the pool into a haunted house once
     or maybe we dreamed it   in the cold snap.
I don't know what to eat. This isn't the best place
     to preview illusion   and it's easier to write than to listen.

Remember how I walked with nothing?
    The big church glowed red
leaves turned overnight
        corsos kept cutting off.
                    I wanted to build but I couldn't move
                        and you said I smoked too much
                    as we waited for the drunk to have
                        the undertaker's baby
                    and I didn't like how
                        you faced it or death.

HOUSE OF WAX / HUSKER RED

I dream money comes
in an envelope written in Western font
    like a long-lost rogue father
        badness becomes   badness in badlands and learning
                    the blackness
        badness in learning   a venison daughter   a too-soon semi-waste.

    You apologize for your gender in natural colors
    then you just lean back   criticize body hair
            you say burnt fur
    too soon and my limitations you love getting punched in the face.

                It probably seems like we're everywhere
                        taxidermy museums   the axe-murder house
                            sucking joints for our sadness
            and it gets a little murky
                in my little mind
                        w/ all the duck decoys
                            the exposure to the weather
                            the shadow effect   the death day hovers
                                my face like a harlot
                            not heart-shaped enough.
You ask why I'm not mourning
        like Dracula's daughter   you pump up the volume
        and why can't we just fuck?
                        You don't watch TV
                    this house is too hollow
so let's just get sad   and wander the graveyard
            hit the stag bar
                    kiss at the stag bar in my blue-black lipstick

but it's not a diary   if everyone writes it
          hemlock soft hard
          baywood close liquid
                              look into my crystal ball
                              you can't see a pore
it's not a chainletter   when it's this derivate
          but don't you feel like my whore
                    tongue on my tongue once
                    drinking from my bloody cheeks?

                    You'll go back to god
                              so your flatbed truck levitates
          I'll dream a soft curse
                    in the murder cabin
          leave the ghost some tobacco   so in comparison
                                        you're moralistic
                    wash my hair before the hayride
                    wash my hair after the frost
                         even in the snowstorm
                              in the black coat
                         I'll go out to show off my legs—

BATHHOUSE OF WAX / ARKANSAS QUARTZ

Have you ever lied? Have you ever lived on the wings of sin are death?
    Have you ever fawned, found your art-deco heaven
diamonds washing up when it rains?

    My fur and skirt burst into flames.
I glance up from my work   expect a man
    with a knife standing there or a crown.
He ties my fake wrists   I'm not leaving the bathhouse
    damn my privacy   I'll fuck the dead chief
spider spider inside her   I'm hot and leaking
you hate me since I'm brave
    or since I sit   on the face of the girl
        at the rock shop   lick bauxite
in the alien light   of an art-deco night
    the salt-scoop of the bathhouse
sweating it out   as if you can be saved.

He ties my fake wrists   we burn holy standards
the ghost of my manicure
    but have you looked at me with lust in your heart
    a mercury rub or a camel twist?
Drugs on the saucer   footsteps   or death wages
    diamonds washing up when it rains
they don't look like diamonds   there's no time for thinking
    flicker faint and thin

          and how does the heat know
      like a monster or an old lamp
          and have you looked at me with lust in your heart
      like something coming inside me?

BATHHOUSE OF WAX /
CENTRIFUGAL TIP-OVER SWITCH

I'm in a bad bad weight of central time/a bad way
      at the Arlington Hotel   it's a dark liquor thrill
it's a kiss from your god   but I don't like my weight or my fate.
      I'm in a bad way   it's a small town
of fire and dolls haunted   by old baseball players
      and I'm thankful for the gangsters
my Olympic bob frizz   my sticky/sinky
      ambulatory fingers.   Call me an absurdist
my process is mess.   I masturbate through the night
      keep caking sour faces   walk my pink bear on a leash.
I need a new highball   or to gamble by Ozark Bathhouse
      or to go watch the sunset   reflecting off bauxite.
My white sheath is bloody   my nails are a mess
      I need a straight man   with curly chest hair
         to follow me on the trail. I pluck him from the trashheap
push his hand down my pants.

         There's room in this room. There's ghosts on the water
crunching the leaves   and I cough up blood
      since nothing is over   speckled like Indian corn
so I piss on the woodline   get a bit drunk
      don't drink enough water to wait
to wade through the bath   do the camel twist
      and my fortune says   life is for the living
taut film-star bodies   universal toga costumes
      and it's clear the water   prolongs frailer lives
         and I find my art-deco heaven
           it has the best scotch
         and the best needle shower.

BATHHOUSE WAX / WEIGHT AND FATE

Somewhere you don't know I'm freezing
walking downtown   on Dead Chief trail
        to be with the monsters
hide in the closed liquor store
        climbing back up to be with the dark
somewhere you don't know.
        Your luck is trying and it needs the vapors
it needs no more orchids   beside the hot iron
        my fortune says   you're killing your organs
my fortune says   my co-star plays the sax
            dime-sized nipples
        my fortune says   overpriced/overspend
                up and down our screwball   war we light candles
you're rubbing mercury on me
            I can't stand/I'll walk miles
to beauty parlor madness   no hot packs allowed
            and there are no connections
to character readings   there are no smaller worlds
        and I found my sickness   in the gymnasium
my glittery bullshit   disguised as a man
        my dumbbell wrapped in leather
cracked in half as I fell   trapeze-baseball snap
        beginning and ending   in Happy Hollow
skin so pink from the hot springs
        you call me a pig   baby bones in my hair
and life's for the living   or murderous culprits
        or the taut made-up bodies
                    but I put on your pajamas
                        hotel burning down
                    but I put on your ghost like the ritz.

BATHHOUSE WAX SNAP

To Lombard is hard.
To be Lombard   for up to ten days
    you go outside   the glow-in-the-dark blood
and a dance seems important
    but it's absurd to wear pink beads to keep the appointment
to drink modern wine when screwtops come too high.
    Say hello to the speakeasy
red-stained hydraulics   soak w/ baseball players
    drink the tureen   of vapor soup at The Aristocrat.

    Hot Springs baseball black
I fuck Lucky Luciano   the ghost of Russ Colombo
    I lift myself   out of the tub
becoming Catholic   as my sleeping pills strangle
    my family ties. I could tighten this compress
of time on my forehead   ditching the nadir
    my naked bod   my forehead lines
and why aren't the bathhouses open at night
    marine architecture   his funeral flowers.

    I dreamed of a snake   fake wrists
and his house   on bathhouse row
    and the rapist would really   have to be something
to climb up these hills after me
    and if you really believe in chaos
this is only paranoia   but it's hell to be afraid
    of fox skulls and vodka. The foxes plant
their own gardens   and I stay in them so long
    little mole bones get caught in my hair.

GOD BLESS THE HOGS

I live in these woods   of useless crime
            of useless time   I paint my nails thick
won't pay money to climb   the old mountain tower.
            You made me think of a play kitchen
orange-tipped with pink   when you asked how people
      who don't have sex live. The heat toward the heart
will molest any wounds. I leave my keys and my kidneys
      by Kidney Spring.   I wriggle out of white satin
ask campfires harder.   I want to believe in the afterlife
            so you'll buy your crypt next to me.
      I want to revolve   past the shit in the woods
but actually I'm thoroughly depressed. I put on a topcoat and I pray
with a twang
      my black on black bleat poisoned redundancy.

I burn incense lamenting the vagaries
      of my blood-smeared broken-heart face. It looks like the clay
      of the monster mother   in that ghost story
bright red eyes the size   of your silver dollars.
      I've become that kind of girl. I might sneak booze in
as my stomach bloats like a moll.
                  We don't have a mother   the camping girls gloat
                  We beat the drum   couldn't care less

42

In this town I hear owls in the bootlegger's lounge
        and I miss The Vapors   big bands used to play
            and my sign is blank   but, hey, there's the man
        with the cross that says *God*   *loves you this much*
            across it horizontally and its arms aren't that long.

WE BATHE THE WORLD /
BATHHOUSE PAGEANT

Success is all hollow   I wear big purple glasses
          and your dirty sheet like a toga.
     I'm not leaving the steam.
I'm not leaving the electronic   massage torture chamber
          but you can send me a message   on the elevator
          via machine:
walk back to your cabin/someone will kill you so they can go live there.

                    Haunted jazz babies   haunt best in hog pink
but I dream of the smell   of the old yellow phonebook
     I dream of a high chair, playing school
               crushed velvet hollow   add risk and suspense
               lavender jabbering   Al Capone grabbing
     my ass on a bench. That bird is hoarse.
          I can hear owls from town
     and I feel your claws   your namesake steps
          and down my back   your slap-lack of narrative
               your slimy kiss.

You're eating an apple and I'm afraid
          of tight jockey shorts   the fake rattle snake
               stuffed with the light stuff and how do I come across
above and beyond and below all the blondes

                        and the breasts that make war
                        and there's always been orange and range
and there's always been   ballistic missiles
        muscles and hunger   no teeth
    and now I just notice   because I love him
    and now I just fuck   in the backroom
        at The Vapors and weep for the last of the Hollywood meteors
    then you lower me down
        wrapped in loose bloody towels to the cooling room.

BATHHOUSE OF WAX /
MADCAP COMES ACROSS

If you really believe in chaos   then this is paranoia
        pretty god drawn and quartered
sometimes I bundle   avoid any distraction
        vow to leave early   dream of flowered waters
                but now it's white pills   and the holy standard's
getting fucked against bauxite   flat numerology
                clawing the mahogany bar
they brought in one piece on the train car.

        My brocade   my high-waisted   velvet pajamas
the dampness of the cabin   making me sick
        soft numerology   making you slick
too many old fashioneds   so let's sit at the campfire
        and say thank god the jockeys
don't have a key   but the hounds still drag me
toward my crystal ball crack-up   Carole ends in an *e*
        and I'll have a reason   even on the dead beach
to turn back the clocks   pin-curl my hair.

        I found my art-deco heaven   in the Predicta TV.
I found my oasis   it broke in half
        profane angel on your fingers
true confession slumming   or dogging for quartz
        the centrifugal way   talking ghost stories
ash blonde in the arsenic   blood and lead spring.

One spring is not   electromagnetic
and I'm the tarantula girl   high-hatting on caskets
      and I'll hike   to your liver or kidney spring
my pubic bush like the forest   queen velvet of rabbits
      messy orange paint opaque
before Florida was invented.

            I'll be buried in a sportscar
                        the formaldehyde will wipe
            right off your fingers
                        since comedy is a long-shot
            I don't need   the tragedy face.

HOUSE OF WAX / REWIND

Go outside for your fifty   seconds of daylight
    vodka in your coffee hit hate/saturate.
What girl doesn't like bite   blonde-black and pink
    a hit parade recovery or Dracula's daughter
      in your bloody-lit lily-print negligee?
You want to be madcap   but what is it really?
    You had a friend   in winter once.
When she gave you half the necklace
    it was like getting her peridot moon
her period/bump-cherry faith.

    You promised yourself you wouldn't leave lace
in her secret slit.
    You promised yourself you'd go out in the daylight
voluminous shampoo   or color-change arsenic
    good and dependable   to go with your mood
of half-achievement   half wolf-shredded sheets
    and you hate all your sisters
      when in this cold you should love them—

HOUSE OF WAX / ACHES AND PAINS

It will be bad news   but go ahead, take a walk
       make your own pizza
like it's the same   as snorting cocaine   in the Arbor Day Plaza
    or racking up red steps
        under the watertank
or how you mock Dracula   w/ bad hair and a flat chest
       bat bikinis   black dresses
    and not enough jewelry.

Vampires live   on red sauce or thick venison
    rotting amber in heat
       and you don't even listen to me
     just send the obituary   but what could the cat music
       in my scrapbook mean?

You lock me in the zoo   my soft leopard stole losing heat
      or you lock me in the wax house
or you spot me at the restaurant
    and stare atavistically   murmuring *sister*
burn me in street
       say his death means the ass-end
        of good times, the 50s
       your fancy grief.

In this town full of scarecrows   gold wallpaper, trains
    men kissing from trucks
        give me dead country magic.
   I buy a strange ring to put on and get sick
   I pray with a twang   walking the earth
      undead in Nebraska.

LIVE TO TELL

Put your money in the dollhouse
     it will say whom you'll marry
put your money on the axe blade
     and no one will care
or put your money in a dead duck
     and hand it to a cop
in your rush to be eccentric   an erotic blonde gong.

I cannot rush but I want that cult following
     or I want to watch trash
with the devil in the bathroom
     urging me toward the trails
the electric planchette.

I lock the rooms with a stone when you're not home
     the boy with bad eyes and a limp takes my ticket
shit out or shut out
     or the boy rings my orange lipstick.
Put your money in his mouth
     and he'll sew a ruffled blood blouse
     or a bone daydream
or the fact is there's really worse things to have
     than fingerplay long and strong
than praying to pay for it.

So much hunger at the murder house   abandoned clay pigs
        I rearrange the alphabet blocks
ask if this town is all slaughter
desperate for bread and physical comedy
        hang on the answer
a deader grandmother haunting the trees
        in my flapper beads
or it's a ghost cow   since every once in a while
        the cows want to moo at the moon
and every once in a while I think you'll kill me
        to drape my middy blouse on a scarecrow.

YOU WRECK ME / HOUSE OF WAX

Sure we had nostalgia   it was all good and dead once
        it was all god and unusual transparency
too much eyeliner   in twilight sympathy.
          I hid silver knives and opened all the channels
        and then you drug me, said
the next eight years will be this day
hanging sweaters in the basement   crying off my makeup
          and I haven't felt a thrum
on my long scar in a long time   or the gummy baby blanket
        but I could burn the flowered box of doll clothes
I could run through prairie murders
        in nothing but my bra
I could make a change purse   for your psychopathic costume
        or I could learn the Charleston   come screaming in your pocket
crush my bloody panties   sucking on a turnip
        or I could leave the house   have you follow me
like a too-long chase scene   eat a sandwich yes or no.

        But I dreamed him and me
on a hill above the river   my teeth were cinna-snapping
        right down to his soft asscheeks.
He hung a dead fish up   like a leitmotif
        asked me about the floodplain
then asked me to curse the floodplain
          and maybe I could really
wrap my legs around him   like a gold-heeled Clara Bow

and then maybe I could make him   run me by the mortuary
       then fuck me on the traintracks in a cape.
      We'd be falling for each other
in front of all the lace-lined coffins
       and we wouldn't have a chance.

HOUSE OF WAX

I don't understand   lacy ambiguity
      paper, clock, leather
how to be special   or, poisoned, transgress
      so let's walk the cemetery.
I'll pass the busroutes   baroque spiderwebs
      fulfill my daddy fantasy
              brush back your rough hair
      pretending you're Bela Lugosi.

I know the story. Sundown's a beauty
      but you're just a baby and I want some zest
chest hair better than ash blonde
before scar distinction   spatterdash on the floodplain
      a pink bloodstained stuffed horse.

I light the candle   smells like ghost tobacco
      smells like the boys never got close.
I try to be fine   with great lies and a fireplace
      but I can't leave the room
      answer your household questions.

I spin the dial smoothly   get to the river
long trains on the floodplain   get to my illusions
      loving the flame within soft curls and tweed.
      I dream the pool open in late October
but the smell of bleach is existence
      so I mop up the scene.

The vampiress on the 80s TV show
        wears crushed purple velvet
        drinks her blood afraid of AIDS.

I don't want to apocalypse
        my eyes on the lighter
Dracula song and/or Dracula shadow
        I don't want to apologize   burn some of my bleached hair.
        The old TV's broke   I keep hearing its snow.

                        ·

WEIGHTS AND MEASURES

I never promised you a chokeberry   or a cheap Grecian costume.
I like you but not quite that much
     but this will end with a skeleton   a ceramic pig
or a rock garden   every day firefighting
     river-smart and eager
dressing up dead possums   as dandies or brides.

A man reads a map at the parish
     as if he's the river   better than me.
I'm wrapping blankets around the trees
     climbing wood casements   slicing the crescents
but if you live with me I'm not safe.
     I'm not a baker   I exist like a ghost
I see the night scenes   through CCTV in the day
     filtered by ashes   then I can't go home.

Hayride ridiculous   apple bobbing and crosses
     extinguish my time
and I guess I'll clean up   know the cheap Grecian costume
     is so I'll have a shroud   at the end
to run through the graveyard.

But first there's wallpaper   a cozy star bar
     a side car   a falling barometer
a sixth anniversary   a stake in the heart
     high small and globular.
But first there's a tad of fresh air

forced socialization
the flame within white gown
    the blonde bun in my hair
        when you say *you were his gold girl*
        you were his favorite
I wish I could be happy
    I want to be natural
        you bumped me out of first place
        this should be comforting

But aren't we all moving toward our final days anyway?
    and when it came to his death he was philosophical
and can't I call you later from the bedroom
    when I use this antenna   to tune sexy frequency?
Right now I'm engaged with his ghost's heavy breathing.

HOUSEHOLD / OLD GOLD

You ask me what's your trauma
  as I rob you of your cheap scotch
in my silk sailor pajamas
  as I creep down there to fuck you
already drunk on vodka
  but it takes time to know a place
like a leather anniversary like a fortune-teller's forecast
  or a desert-mountain smash up
    or a stark affair.

Comedy is harder the candle is my crutch
  but in the Venice Beach short
let's just focus on my blonde crotch
  and I'll stand in the town square
of this town that's not my own
  let homeowners fly their flags
at half-mast marcelled ghost.

The one time I looked good smooth smoke on the throat
  my midriff exposed leopard sex
a magic fur like a roadside attraction
  I stumbled drunk through screwball city
    and all the girls said *drag her*
  drag her through the blood-muck
underneath the roadster
  rip her face off with the roadster.

Now you make the best of me
     I'll make the best of you
return the bad luck bloomers
     the wind-up doll narration
the haunted radio.

Now you climb up the red-lit watertank
     to jack off on my sweater   wrap me in your black lace
to say *you have to have a steady hand* *to find your proper station*

LOMBARD ONE

It feels like a waste to make blonde hair so beautiful and then sleep all day
    and not finish your life   with a pink horsey
but the dark is so good
    it feels like a roar or a scar
and there is this part of me   that hates coming out
    in a pencil skirt, crayon   on the backs of my legs.

Dinner feels like a waste
    so go to the river sit   and think about winter
       how you'll tremble too much
    to open the door with a gun

             how first there was a death hoax
          and then a real death
           then the comfort of trains
           then trains going off the track
        how I hated the cows and the phase
   a lovely lady on the prairie/an impressive   conspiracy theory
         nothing sacred haunting
         nothing sacred hating
      a home-sized asteroid   in a town not my own

    and I need to unstick myself
exist for something   over the flood
    exist for something   rain or blue plates
beyond salads, light drugs.

It feels like a waste to make blonde hair betrayal in the flattest city
coming in rivalry   a pink suit and gloves.

        Let me do the windmill   or let me keep sleeping
        no sunset tonight   under the roller rink
            in Shenandoah, Iowa
the second edition   of small-town tragedy
        or, white blonde, heavy lidded,
the second screen test
        then it's a question of who owns the humor
                the screwball ancestress   faster and looser
                        or who owns the horror?

HOUSE OF WAX / CINNASNAP

I could say   a worm in apple
    don't make my black lips blue
always done up   or add up
    they'd have to put chicken wire
between you and my hips on the stage.
  I communicate sadness   red lip and tips
since shit will happen   in a bloodstained negligee
    and Bela Lugosi's baby
looks like a mini-Dracula.

They say fingernails are the key to your health
    gothic, anemic   and how did sadness go?
and I had a dream   about a man with a pool cue
    strapped to his back
and my lack of birth control   and my lack of headspace
    in the weather of Satan and white satin dresses.

Sadness goes viral   the same man driving by
    in a vampire mask
  the hunger of the tarantula girl
inside the B movie   but spiders are a sham
    and I want my nails plastic
want to dig up his body   with a plastic Halloween pail
    reading his obituary
       make it a wolf or a bear
then follow his healthy   still-growing nails
    past the men to the traintracks.

BAD BRIDGE, DEVIL RED RUMBLE SEAT

I was the new kind of blonde
    appetitive longlegged automaton   a miniature sheep farm
in Brownville, Nebraska.
              I don't trust what I've done
                    but have you done it with a hot water bottle
                        a fear of your fall stalker
                    or any regularity?
              I was the new kind of bride
    I gave up being pure   with any knack for California gold
                a kind of unconscious
                    scotch and soda superstition
                a fair woman acts dark
    I gave myself over   to two dudes with pool cues
        strapped to their backs
                    I gave up my future   at Meriwether Dredge.

        My future starts at 10:27
                    red watertank glows   wind factory dark
        before he fucks me, he asks
            do you have any interest
        in a car wreck that will take   the skin off your face?

Screwball queen masquerading   as queen of the harlots
                    erecting my high heel
        exactly in front of the witch jail
                    a kind of unconscious superstition
                    a thin line between kissing and suicide

I'll enter the dinner party dressed like Madam Satan or Norma Shearer
false eyelashes maybe.
I'm afraid of the party   but your id will give me a ride.

SCREWBALL IN BROWNVILLE

screw loose I hear you above me
     in your black prairie study
high fear and spiced tea
     fever windy but death
would still be so smooth on the throat
     but the ghost smoked the last cigarette
left me vodka shots   said *take out your orange fangs*
     cry into the mush
               write me automatically
     or spread your ass open
     under the cock of the plains.

Not a brunette but I gave advice once
   the smell of yellow phonebooks
     all the dark electrons
  I rode a pink bike in an oval
said don't plop your ragdoll   on my leather desk
     but what's the use
  if you can't control ends
     hang a blue noose in the back room
or run out in your leopardskin jacket
     all the ashes blowing around you.

On the wall the pioneers
on the floor the cosmic energy
       I'm the bathing suit beauty
       with the long-shot mangled face

chaste, reobsesssed   at Meriwether Dredge
       the old soundtrack   at the traintrack
the botched surgery
       and you can change a lock or crack an egg.

You ask me what I'm into
       and I pull up my tight skirt
you ask me if I'm dirty
         a virgin playing possum
       who had to learn blue talk

I don't know what I'm into
       the shortness of two-reelers
        or clacking toward that back room
      in open-toed spat shoes
       or just not being wrecked.

TRUE VALUE

How to crack down   transgress empty space
       corn, so much storage on the flood plain
how to worship this quiet, this time.
       Something comes out of the comfort of trains
when you put all your poison   into one place
       and run to the river.

I wish it were colder   I wish musk hunker-downer
       for this tartan couch
red phone on the wall   transitional
       for this special sequence.

Everyone says   she needs a retreat   mostly just to touch
       mostly just to come in   call it a den
so she fucks the taxidermist   sterile as a dead dad
       each extinct chicken   stuffed, an achievement
when he gets tired enough   he'll rip his feeding tubes out
       say *this is my house*   *but there's a dumbwaiter*
          and my skin will hang off my skull.

Here's where we put the eyes
       here's where we put the cellophane   we make into the lake.
My sweater is jacquard   with your phone number
       dive-bombing beetles   in the witch tense.
          The door is a guard
       strappy shoes and someday   I'll let the ghosts come to me
strappy shoes and someday   I'll remember it gladly

no screens on the windows
and on the flood plain   how many trains
       the language of flowers or the more profane language of stones.

FREIGHT VALUE / SCREWBALL TWO

Suddenly I'm obsessed   with—bridge out—the river
        the sad Mary Astor   with the house-arrest anklet
pink-haired lookalike in pink amulet
        appellation/apparition   what she does in this city
afraid of the river   burning the church for insurance, pink ice.

Say I have a mission   no longer half mast
        I read the map backwards
                a numb tree adventure   1,000 cups of tea
the scarecrow broadbacked   singing I'll singe my hand
        a simple question of candles   of letting the air in
my ego illuminated   too big for fiction.

        Did you hear a commotion   a skull with skin over stone?
Sometimes I think I'm all right
        shiny, unmystical   but I have been summoned
                            by a clock that is lying
        to faint in the woodsmoke   or on the woodline
                but I want to stay   iron my dress on the mirror.

I feel like a tree of missed opportunity
        sleek legs in the leaves
                ill-starred scar on my face.
I turn this way   away from the slasher
        want to believe when you say
everything has its time so just wait
        but I've torn my white robe
                and I'm missing a klonopin.

AUTUMN KISS / MEAT LUST

screwball-long walks   apologies for your gender
      smearing pesticides on my lips in the haze
kids climbing the tree   not turned blood enough
        still I thought we had something
lying down side by side   in hay on the traintracks.
        I'd braided my skeleton   planned a new planet
   quick money   lips and tips   matched like a floozy
           touched up my moody cinnasnap roots.
          We said we could predict
        each other's death day   the antique phonestand fallout
          the foldout bar in the car
               my sex-antic slant   or the noose in the room
          but all the human noises   were in someone else's yard.

His truck bed was full   of muddy duck decoys and booze
           and what demons when I rip
       out this bloody heartland   in my deep-blue nightie
           in my half-off cape.
You say I get lucky   that I can't sustain narrative
      master and slave
                 so I drive to the river
         past the man with the shotgun
            I drive in the corn   so kiss me bye-bye
               I'll rise once a year
              since this town is mad
          for blonde carcasses dressed up like scarecrows.

MADCAP / THE DRACULA SCRAPBOOK

It became a time   of touching up nails
fastidiously   the search for resonance
       in today's emergency
the forcing yourself to the end of the murder
       the self-guided tour
or railroad fever, willful thinking
       horseshit and scars
and I cannot say   I get the folklore
            one subversion a month
       butter rings in the soup
the no time, the tap class in Omaha.
            I don't like the wood waiting
       but it's not you I snap at
the putting away   but turn the heat down
       pine needles stabbing me
            in the child-sized coat closet.
I am not the one   to start the oscillation
       with the small dog on Water Street
all the way to Nemaha
       but I hide all the lipsticks
       and I once thought the dredge
was a person.
       I photograph better
in my *Girl from Missouri*
       wide black and white hat
and you ask if I can send you
       a penis of the plains

while men try to be big with religion.
  Light-haired girls look the best
in soft icy colors
  and every once in a while
I want the moon and get tired of hating the flame.
  Every once in a while
I want to be nude   in art-deco newness
  change the color
change the veil   between me and depression.
  There's nothing left but getting laid
drinking bloodsmoke on late-night TV
  a bad taste in my mouth
but this isn't rock bottom
  and is it hunting season yet?
A cold sky   a white-tailed white light?

THE LONG SHOT

DID SHE GO TO HELL?
YES, AND THEY CALLED IT HOLLYWOOD

It's love I'm after   or monkey business
          or this river on the floodplain
      but I think I've found my ghost.
          She's getting drunk on this last day
      she says I smoke too much
          she says I am bankable   I better behave
      but am I tough enough?
          She's the last of the It girls
      and she is small enough   to slide through
                the rails of her sickbed.
          This town, houses hollow
              too close together
          pink triptychs   pink tricycles parking outside
              and on the sidewalks rusted hairpins
          my blood-stained Draculette cape.

I killed Rita Hayworth   she felt too frothy.
          Was it Carole Lombard
      or Constance Bennett
          in the scene of the scarred factory mirror?
      It's too hot in here   for the longlegged deer
          but I asked her how
      I sucked down all the vodka.
          I did not light a candle
              but I did ask her how

I sucked down that Halloween sunset
before the ghost I found
turned into a bat.
Suddenly I'm vomiting
all over the cornfields
suddenly I'm shedding
all my extra weight in your cornfield
but aren't we all equally talented?

Suddenly I'm pissing   in my white jewel-toned nightie
behind all spooky pines
missing when late-night TV
was like another universe
color-changing arsenic   shrinking my waist
madcap and darkness
the blue-black route a dead rooster
you flip me over
and fuck me   how we hide from police—

SPARKLE PLENTY

For best results, choose a prediction
          damaging fungus   existing in plain sun
hair tangled   no cosmic   layer of irony.

For best results, close off   or else walk through the pain
    walk there in a day   your blue skirt, hips busting
your awkwardness not enough   to keep you away.

        Why did you say   to exist to make money
      and drink champagne was ugly?
          Why didn't you say   Harlow's hair falling out
      when living past her seemed impossible?

For best results, the iconic   white dress and the virus
      a dual suicide   me & Harlean
    in an in-between decade
a walk across Venice Beach   intravenous barbiturates.

    Why did you say   a skull and two fingers
to get off, clear crystals   and blondeness all over
      to lie in a stone circle   outside of Bakersfield
a martyr for Palm Springs   both lip-sets shot wet?

      For best results, what are we doing this for?
Moving forward through a false childhood
    through a decade of me is a tease
    blood-matted   bad dye jobs   blonde doppelgangers

like deer, the long-legged divorcees
overwhelmed by the drugs and the gloves and the clothes.

For best results, close off.   They say if you see
your twin lose her head then you die
          and the caps on the Venice Beach waves
              sparkle like toothpaste

essential tremors   giggly with bubbles
     a large church   paper lovers
cheaters and cameras   making me cheep

     pillowslip satin   serving all masters
          better than nothing   and abducted X-rays
               for more than just bones.

AUTO-MONROE / PRE-AMPLIFIED SPLICE

or a saint's day   a deep forest precursor.
I went through a phase when I was better than dead
    an automaton deep in the Poconos
my asshole burning   deep in cheap jewelry
    a bubbly hottub   other end of the camera.

All success comes from struggle   curly-haired candles
    Hollywood futures   in suitcases cascade.
        Is it possible you know I'm a liar
        posthumously recuperated and just look at the pictures?
    And I read your forest compulsively
      all death comes from plaid dresses
      a black ribbon at the neck
    and I must have pearly nails to succeed in the city.

When I go into occult mode you call me unclean
    kitchen witch/crack the book open
a woman in crystal   too weak to think.
    I should feel guilty   for my lack of interest
in living history   that fear that you'll trace me
    that you want the end of the war
that I want the war and an egg cream.

    Who's to say I was naked   or nude in the woods
surrounded by dead chickens   vintage inspired
      and twenty electrical moons
my platinum hair, an ultra-short-wave receiver

modernity, a series of setbacks.
I went through a phase   where my death was better than anything
    but the newspaper said   stop hiding, start living
      so I rolled myself into their light.

STAR '80

Playmate '80. Becoming the platinum screen
    for the horsepills of the 70s
the failings of democracy
      the sordidness of wanting   a Russian sable jacket
        in a spy coat   dripping cream.

Gaudy wheel of fortune grinding   but he said I got off cheap
    my white lace off-the-shoulder
both lipsets metal wet.
    I'd learned to naked roller skate
smearing oil inside me   that first night at the motel
    everyone a holiday.

And which prize will you pick
    the blood-red jet   the modern kitchen
the witch, almost escaped   the swamp burial in mud
    the fly me to the moon   and jam it in my blank?

To hear him think today
    the trash is in your bloodline
and men do not make passes
    as I layer on felt panties   pig slit, no violet tan
hide my bush and laugh.

The script gets rewritten   in the virus of night
        who knows it ends in guts and money
      a bloody broomstick   squeaky bondage?
He says the star that breaks the playmate's back
      is that you were stupid

but what I know is stardom
        is cock-pink supplication
        taking houses you can't haunt
        and wet forevers in your mouth.

THE SCRIPT GETS REWRITTEN

In Grand Guignol   color's the enemy
except for that one play   w/ blood and balloon.
        Gun-shy, we answer the drinks
in order of inquiry   live anachronistically
        my pubic hair itchy   outside the bone.
            I hit you with my order
my pirate palette   my cloisonné bouquet.
        I cry silver tears since the grand dame of Pigalle
may have lice   but a platinum blonde can stop time.
        Guide my name-saint across death
I'll sleep in this prince's   bed like a ship
until kingdom come   leave the scent of wild pussy and piss
        at the coconut club.
                On the remarriage radar
        open your mind. Order wine like a French girl
the peculiarities of time. No White Russians no heavy-lidded cats' eyes
        no undertone pink.
            I have a whole half-life
before I exit routine   and I might end up dead   dark in the bathtub
        a GI's bandage in my throat   flashbulbs exploding
or I have been summoned by a clock that is lying
        the pretty parade.   I cry silver tears
look at that stained glass window.   It becomes real.
            Is that the future or is that Milwaukee?
All I do is play showgirl, the oddity.

PILLOWSLIP WHITE AND / OR BLONDE SCREENS

Say hot or cold movie   loosely based on the death of your starlet
      or loosely based on a death star
racking up bracelets   slow days of nothing.
The craze started in New York   (sage, basement occult)
      and moved toward the dark trees
blondes posing nude   by the pool or the moon
      blondes projected at night   under werewolf clouds
on the side of the uncle's garage
      but the little girl hangs   handkerchiefs on the clothesline
      nascent during the day   or wheels her bald doll
across cul-de-sac glow.

      They called her the new Garbo   cradled her when she posed
next to the igloo ice cream shop.
      He said, I know   I know in my bones
what you can do   and then she got fat
      and they sent her home   writing her lover in black
      force-fed her sun and a bathing cap
both depressed and platinum.

She smashed all the records   burned all the dresses
      said hot or cold movie
stretched herself on the wheel   her sagging breasts bound

                  a modest house, wrought iron
                  pills washed down with ice cream

84

and in the backyard, a rusted swan gondola
and Monroe's death pronounced
      from the heart-shaped radio
as lightning struck nine miles away
      and we acted it out
all that August compulsively
      twinging in our legs
under the sunporch
      or under the blanket
where life seems so short and so long.

MADCAP / CABIN FEVER

My habits are bad   I don't know what's at the wheel
  sleeping long days   dreaming dead deer
    or deer horns or nothing.
Alive alive-o   forms a good number
  crumbling old letters   feast or fiesta
but this blue candle   does not smell like fall
    and I can't tell if the groan
    is my home or an animal
or why I am walking this ice storm alone
  devil gloves and pink puffballs
     the starlet zone code
  in a world without love when this could be Hollywood.

  The fine-fingered winged girls
black lips/silent o's
  but I don't have enough time between assaults
to let my hair grow back natural
  so I find icy playboys
the ways their lips tingle with scotch
  give the white high heels another shot
   vow I'll be productive
drink less or more   little sips   vow I'd be better
   off in lands of moors
  since I can't stand your voices.

      Introductions are worthless
you know my winged liner
      another faux fur   and this is the dusk
through which I tote a glass lantern
      through money and glitter
and Mari Lywd gloaming
      and there's not enough coffee
to mix with the liquor   before we jump in the roadster
      or the river.

In the film I'm the dead aunt
      and the contemporary ghost of myself
too afraid to move   and I'm afraid I'll lose
         men, cigarettes, or electricity
           my cologne smells like moss
        and I'll find places to hang
     my photos of Jean Harlow's grave
           and we'll meet in the bathroom
          and fuck in our bathrobes
      as the topcoat smooths everything.

MADCAP / WHEN SHE GETS LIT
SHE GLOWS

I can't stand the tell-all   the rosary ghosts
        Harlean holding the wreath.
    I wear a black leotard   look for an excuse
feel like I deserve   some vestige of sophistication.
        You know how you feel
           pink washing out
       you know if your ear's blowing up.

You know psychodrama   shampoo, finger wave
      heat greeting you   empty hours in the empty house
        twisting the ribbon   like pregnancy.
You know the girl story   and even cat-eyeliner
      and lack of lace   a woman alone
bulky not delicate   the lack of turning in focus.
     I turn on my hip like the old paper Christmas tree
a blue ten-speed bike for each leg
     I lie like my story comes from the dead
a mechanical lamp that could knock us both out

and hey I have a name for the bare shelves at sunset
     I have a name for the beer you won't drink
and how you won't drive anywhere.
     I have a name for my bare self
        like in the present   wherever you are
      with your greasy hair   you cover your ass like a bullet.

And I don't want to walk   I just want to cry
      I'm bored by the world   the old TVs and mirror spirits.
        I don't feel like I'm worth it
        and I'm so drunk I can't even
     make my way to the bedroom
        and I'm so drunk I don't even
know my own face   as we vacuum out babies
    we vacuum out graves.

MADCAP / PURE ICE

I used to believe in horror and silence
    the vampiress in the wicker chair
with the purple cushion on the talk show
    or bobbing for apples   with Uncle Dracula
sweating blood in a barrel   a blue hippopotamus mask
    the cage in the room   the old flute and someday
I promise a clean smell   the promise of urgency.

    I used to get tired of seeing my dry nails
got tired of the new snow   the hashtag cold snap.
    In the dead town they trusted me so much
they let me live in the waterless home
    and all the walls echoed   and I turned
the petrified radio   to sad jaws and diamonds
    added glitter to the deer head still warm
and the cat clock that never stopped ticking
    a gold ghost on my cranberry nails
my booze and headaches   a femme fatale in faux fur
    and the vampiress is my grandmother
my high-waisted panties
    I watch gameshow after gameshow
    and never have sex.

MADCAP / FEMME FATALE

Is there anyone I can tell   how horrible these blues are?
        Your 4 o'clock bell   says I do it for boredom
                in my baby blue trench coat
sit at the teatable trailblazer   wait for the haze.
        My brain is cooped up   I don't want to look
touch up my roots   sit under the dryer
        my fingernails painted   peel-off cherry candy
red like a toddler
            but manicures look so gracious
and I love baby brushes   your raw egg and brandy
        and rings on my fingers   running through mud
creek-cross like a deer   straddling you
        after you take away   my crystal-clear topcoat
my identification   shedding my horn and my evidence.

I want to be gifted but I have no habits
        I think of orange fur   cross earrings, orange leather
being the sexy secretary on our playdate
        the butterfly brooch from Australia   brown tartan
how you think too bright for the camera.
        I'm bored. I'm compulsive.
I buy all the bracelets in their rotting red boxes.
        need a new year/made for each other
need nude nails, gold-fitted spaces.   I think of the cinema
        wet feet, pneumonia then I live in an iron lung
lacy, flesh-colored bed jacket
        and I hide the gun in my ass   bad judgment

and don't call the censors   and I think how the killer
      hid in an iron lung for years for revenge
and how every gangster movie
       ends at a banquet with a carnation wreath
and a bloodbath.

MADCAP / BIG SHINY

So far from our mind   and so close to velour
      Xmas trees still up
with styrofoam hearts   slight cellulite
      poodle skirt and martinis
          but nobody sees me
nobody wants to hold   the thought in their head
      the skeleton on their Predicta TV.
The TV is a behemoth   in your basement bar
      I drink blood to ride   and rise in rank
on the blow-up champagne bottle.
      I think of the platinum rocking horse babies
how I could fall asleep in TV sleet and freeze
      but let me put on your show
spicy and alpine.   Daddy, I wear the costume
      for nine dreadful hours
          confused by numerous hearts.
I pick at the scene   wonder how/if I'll die
      all my lives black and pink
before go-go dancing
          lights up my legs.
I can't stand being smashed in this sign-time
      the big clock in Kiev and hands on my belly
unapologetic   protecting invisible sweethearts
      reaching up for the strings
never promised/remembering   how pink ice can kill you
          outside the warm restaurant
      lined with dead chickens.

Harlow before me kept getting married
        ears pricked up   she put on
             an overbite show
      black makeup   soft rabbits
her face in a heart
           and I always choose
     silent flicks over noir
this time a plaid coat and Victorian gaiters
       and my wish for an hourglass-shaped swimming pool
and a mint manicure that outlives me.

MADCAP / MAKE MUSIC FOR MODERNS

I'm losing steps   too tired to care
     transmitted three times
canary wires   and master/slave station.
          I want to start being
          the cold kitten flick   of booze and machine
     the sultry lounge singer
society sleuths   suspect on the thrill boat.
          In this my film noir
          it can't get any darker.   I try to watch the tell-all
          to no avail   I put my money on my eyeliner
     for security/serenity
          blimp my lips with tissues
     Gloria Grahame style.   I have a certain elegance
          I don't take down my Christmas tree
               I'm afraid to go outside
     but my kindred spirit   is the man with three antlers
          and I masturbate   I watch
     the glitter on my fingers   outside the dead mall.
          He has a huge cock
     but all I have is surface   scratched palms and track marks.

MADCAP / WE TOUCH BASE AS HARLOTS

If I could just get in the habit   finish introspection
       the old psychic sidekick   my absurd hats.
I'm playing a ghost of myself   as orchids suicide.
       I have been patronized
now I want to get paid.
       I am my father's daughter
drinking scotch to watch the Christmas movies
       before they go away.
We're warned of the azimuth
             all the roses are icy   all the corpses frozen
       with your swampy crystals
and domestic scenes are so cozy   if red cheeks are colorized.

I strap on my snowshoes
       throw myself at playboy Christ
if I could just get in this habit
       timelined and pre-amplified
say coffee makes me me again
       but really it's blue drugs
the miracle cure   candelabras are everywhere
       mermaid pink nails   and depressive hedonia
becoming a virgin   a kitten again
             by the radio tube
the coupling loop   my hand in my tender blonde crotch.

What's the significance   when you don't want to sparkle
        or pray with old notes   the cat-crunch
              the everlast manicure.
We deem this a Paris divorce
              after the deer   after the soft
        after the lost frost of Christmas or cinema
assigned seats in Vienna.
        I give you credit for the mildly pornographic
milky prototype.   I give you credit
        for leaving the house as Harlow or Lombard
pink cheaters   white sun.

        You say the palette of blush is too much
but make-up's my escape   as is smoky pink faux fur
              and when you do your nails
              when you wash your hair
touch up your roots each Sunday
        God save your manicure
this will take on a texture   like foreign cinema
the fair woman acts dark   a depth I can't articulate.

PICTURE-IN-PICTURE /
OUR DANCING DAUGHTERS

How do you handle   starting out late
     past the time of the platinum wink
the sadness of the frozen blonde   Xmas tree fever-tease
          the sadness of fortitude?
     Any process is aging. Any process is weird.
I feel no need to stomach   cheap cigarettes, purple ink
          I don't know how to pace
     bondage, cryonics, or tears.
I feel no need to share   a living doll story
     a birdcage-shaped ass
long-legged nightclub dancers
     sex shame or my pubic hair.

If I died today, my bones too boozy
     you'd say leave me your gangster
or at least your gangster movies
     you'd sleep all day   say how to fix the broken strap
came to you in a dream.

     If I died today   my stardom surrounded
by a micro-charge   by a bone-in-bone frill
     you'd be well-dressed   collecting eggs
dressed like a moth   I would bind you and blind you
     but this is not my sister   perfect grave
peaceful rain. This is not the longest day.

This is not black-lipped, faux-bobbed
modern maidens.

This is just another me   sans wink in her skin
        calling you daddy   timing my life by the deer
on the side of the road.
        I step in what's rotten   and even my voice
comes in after death   helps you poison your mind.

Say my death is foul play
        say hidden hustler   a freckled relic
            or an optional paradise.
To avoid having your baby I flew into the sun
                or you shuttered my corpse in the rumble seat.

MESSY WIFE / MESSY LIFE / DAILY MOTION

Platinum is my element   and at least I have my health
        vanitas, a diminishing vision.
I'm a novella   or a plaid playsuit
        or they must have devised another name for me
                bone-bed, semi-swine.

Don't dance where you eat. I look at the slop
                understand why women   give up, disappear.
I look in the mirror   see jewelry, no face
            a tramps-in-the-tropics   melodrama, cocaine
        cellulite, sentimentality   coming in stages
            all motives trace   loving or money
        semi-sweet lightning strikes east.
                        I reply with a drink
                don't fuck where you eat.
                        I become more than muse
when attention-seeking's genetic
        I don't want to bathe or smoke cigarettes
        depression that deep. I become more than muse
on one meal a day
                when your porn is greater than my porn
        my sailor dress   my sea-going cat
            the Hollywood fog   the tarp over the sunlight
pink muscles and what?   What are you basing this day on?

I only abide by   black-and-white miniature challenges.
I lie and say   I'm writing a book
I'm buying a haunted apartment
      or I pretend I'm your criminal
      and I lie in a cave   of porcine saints
      where it doesn't stop raining   (fuck me with stalagmites)
            or I'm a fat planet   with rings tilted your way
      and I lie when I realize I already gave it away.

STRANGE INTERLUDE

They say civilize your rituals
    no makeup on the first night
cheeping through black netting
    light a candle, make it better.

Legs open and the clock   and the Dom Perignon
    for the Harlow RIP scene   red dress and bloody kidneys.

          I start to sweat and swell
    when I think of telephones
girls getting picked up   in saddle shoes at Venice
    hair rolled up in bobs   lemon dresses and the flailing cryogenics.

They say exit the abortion and civilize your rivals
    live until the 70s   in a wood-paneled hotel
in Milwaukee lighting candles
         but I dropped out midcentury
      in pert orange capris
   no shortage of sex   syringes or money
     a sordid bikini   but *she was so fit*
    blue lipstick and time   stuck between blunt objects
        and obligations
    now my cognitive dissonance
        a green Pucci shift dress
    no Jayne Mansfield panty line.

They say civilize your bitches   study all the old scenes
                    but I don't like the old scenes
        a little blonde in pink flowers   swinging on a tire swing
                    catching all our tears in a poison ring.

I OPEN UP
LIKE YOUR WORLD IN LEOPARD

Diamonds disappear and there are different ways
      to talk about darkness.
And the psychiatrist says   you're feeling positive
      about the saints' lives   about the dead babies
      under the rose pencil skirt   your mysterious paunch
sex, sweat, and taxes   about the will to collapse.

Think about sadness   peekaboo tomb rules
        long lapses at night
      how your revenge   could not be artistic
      how your hand hurts   from touching yourself
        from watching the jet-setting theme song
    and how the moon lapping   will not understand
    what it means to be beat up or cut up.

Why didn't you say it was ugly
      erase all the photos   the pathos of me, golden blonde?
I exist to make money   temperature dropping
      an hour gone missing   fur stoles and candles
        first day rain/favorite altar.

Children are ugly and I grew up serving
      so many masters   faux-rococo in sticky canals.
      I became epic   tight-skirted   animal magnetism
        my own background hum the sad drugs.

Call it the culture of martyrdom
but I could spot every woman
　　　steeling herself　　　haunting red houses
as vintage porn melted.

PALM SPRINGS /
BOMBSHELL FALLS APART

Messages heaving
    or blonde-lipped
a dark drink in the desert
    and real pain for the sham friends
treating me worse   than ex-husbands
    or box-office poison.

blood-lipped
a Hollywood presence

Raise your hand if your mind
    slips more than lye
you say you're a dog
    jingle to jangle

too tired to think
    no more wanderlust.

What's my totem or Tarot
    all my hair falling out?

messages heaving

There's truth hanging, too   the pre-emphasis circuit
    too dense to depend.

In *The Saturday Night Kid*   I spoke not a word
    insinuating beads   and microwave frequencies
    and the filter was blue.

    You kept carving songs of collapse
    as if you knew so much of the underworld.

BOMBSHELL PLANCHETTE

Tell the saint's calendar
Old Hollywood   bled bleach and ink
     back when we had standards and Saturdays.
Russell dark/Marilyn light
     diamonds hiding behind
the o of the Hollywood sign
     or the men trading coke under the Moulin Rouge windmill
on the Culver studio lot.

Hills burning, I search for phrases
the challenge of childhood generations   a raised swimming pool
          in the center of western hegemony
          in the hollowed-out rot of Palm Springs
that suppresses my synapses   yet makes me cum.

Tell the saint's calendar we need to return to nostalgia
slide the black velvet pyramid
     over Montgomery Clift's collapsed face
     wrap his bloody front teeth in the velvet
          the hip new wave priest not showing us up
     Liz Taylor covered in pulp.

We need to return to nostalgia
the dark picnic shelter   his knuckles inside me
     then gravel inside my knees
          and how I infantilize bleached public hair and blue filter
wrap silver locks   around my own finger

mail them to you   where narrative's squishy
on the road to the Country Club
    where two girls lost their heads in the 60s

sisters of never   too soft on the tongue
      since you have to be hard not to haunt the lane
      in Harlowesque robes
    haunt diamonds and science, say
         we'll make you happy   if not in this world
         at least in the next.

HOW DO YOU KNOW IF
YOU'RE ON THE RIGHT PATH?

I could go back in time   the skin game afraid of the moon.
I could sit in the driveway   at dusk, my talisman
     a friendship bracelet.   I could try to conjure
sex magic   fat cheeks   a sparkler.   I sawed off your braid
     it will help not to feel   nor see this day
wet-handed transgression   sleepy cheapening, sweat
     a powder puff   a playsuit   swingset and the void
circulation cut off after sex.

Forgive me my tranquility.   I pad our past
     with magazines   by the pool naked
shells over my eyes.   A silent film set
     at the grocery store   slow-moving lobsters
sticky semen and froth.

     Hello transgression. I painted my nails
did not get the meaning.   I watched all the play weddings
     then dropped my red compact
the cat in the shadow   the thief threw the dog at the wall.

I sat at the vanity   lip gloss pots melting
     a sad instrument.   You were in love with summer
as the dog resurrected   at the sight of the rabbit
     my pills phosphorescent
the shadow with the wig   stabbing herself.

You say a child's blackmail is distracting
        but it will be fire.   I tie you down   pry open your mouth
the tranquilizers in your throat
        little halfmoons clacking down.

BOMBSHELL / TEENSPLOITATION

I didn't move today   felt the temptation
    felt movie pressure   like I should conjure engines.
I didn't know which candle   pink or white bullshit
    to help the jewel thief's daughter
solve the crime.

I needed a night book   a day book   a maze
    my party   my problem
brass lips   black confetti   the majorette dress
    Clorox and soap and dense days anointed with flame.
I sent the past some evidence
    her curls bleached so carefully
like a Marilyn zombie.   I sent the past some evidence
    you said *we want to see the wig*
       you burned before the murder
    we want to see the cloche hat blood soaked in your distance.
We want to conjure   your ghost sans religion
    want to truss you up   like a dead James Dean—

I'd died before that reel   my spooky action
    her confession.   She became a better actress
at a distance   the new wave.

I could come at any time.   I could cry the dog is old.
    He lost his teeth.   I played three women in the movie
       or one man on TV.

I could use the whip ride   to hook you back in time
      starlet theosophy   shove you to your knees.
You could sit on my grave   I could stick out my hand...

SPARKLE PLENTY TOO

Guilt's a great motivator
what it means to be human   an unwanted pregnancy
    drugged and sleepy all day   what it means to be human
hair frizz and danger   eyes needled blind
    sex on the fritz   what it means to play
     a starving matchgirl   or to play a princess
    drowned in bone with a syringe

or a suicide out the window
   and a man I don't know   is moving his fingers inside me
   saying *radium girls   moon clouds   luminosity*
     and *you could have been one   after your shift*
       glowing in dance halls
     licking paint brushes   to ornament clocks
       then lifting out parts of your jaw.

     You could have been   sailor blouse/saddle shoes
beauty and truth   milky makeup Harlouche
    open your legs   or forced open, your legs
in a blush-colored dress   fucked up against
    the Hollywood sign.

I'm sorry I cannot   keep up with the roots
in our boudoir picnic.
     The man wants to transpose himself over my lover
    our pussies wet   with orange blossom or pet

113

and I'm the girl to turn toward in darkness
in the ghost scene   throwing stars   moving stones
          and we skate on contagions   leave a note in a handbag
               jump into the canyon   Hollywood-making
          the flowers of odor   the daughters of ulcer.

     Stardom seals green beads   planchettes and palms
the glow in my bones. There's a new blonde with pink nipples
     born every second   but they'll all lose their breasts
          or their heads in the end—

TAKE ME NAKED
IF IT MAKES ME REAL AGAIN

No frigate like a book unread and not the energy
    to open a bottle of pills. Everything's triggering
lifting my hair for the vestige   of old-timey stardom
    or with safety scissors   I chop my own bangs.

Heat makes waking hell and I dwell on eyesockets
    and every morning pay the pine trees.
        It all comes down to money and bloodstains.
A needle and a pearled shawl   took the children away.
    Drink the vodka. Fill the bottle with water.
    We mythologize and he says the witch hunt
is most interesting   and the difference between
    us and the animals   is they can't look for meaning.

        Little songs come fast and I find the letter
by not looking back   or it's somewhere else
    and it poisons my shade
    or I empty out the pantry   to rid myself of him
self-sabotage in heart-shaped sunglasses
    or a more intimate god.

Take me naked. I just told the truth.
    The brass heart in the bedroom turned my past over.
I got through bad moments   black bows
    changed my name.   I solved my own crime
with a made-up boyfriend   and a fake cock

        or I solved the crime   during my period
wearing your cast-offs
                or I solved the crime   as I heard a bell ring
                and the truth is
                your carnage   is general knowledge.

MONROE PLANCHETTE

Look in the coffin window
     so much glam   so much sadness
see the little girl's face   (thick cheeks)
     perfectly preserved   and I just need a way
to disappear into Venice
     let go the stripes of time, a tight blue skirt, my mother
        a lacy paper gondola.

     I could haunt Hotel Ocean.
They gave her a fake name   because no other bodies
     left behind looked the same.

     The first It Girl felt the mercury
     shimmer on her tonsils
   the little girls' dead cheek like a cloud
like how do you handle
   the loss of red lipstick and   brains
black cat lanterns   an airplane body
   and how do you handle   starting out late
a Harlow sans the wink   story so heavy
     the script rewriting each night
a red-heart altar to Harlean
     and men don't make passes at addicts

        and I spend money on Pucci
       don't ask for forgiveness
wiping my lips
     but I know the perfect way
to highlight my own face.

MADCAP / MAKE MUSIC I CAN'T UNDERSTAND

The fear of death makes me honest
    skeletonized   but the body in the park
        doesn't lie or deserve it
    and the crazy man with the stick
            scratches *don't go any further*
    in the mud underneath   the observation tower
           and I waste my green eyelashes
and I go to the pond in tight curls, organized.
        I see nary a beaver.
        I sit on the soldier ghost's lap.
I'd like to say   make a child in my name
    the fear of death makes me honest
but both are a lie   and I'd like to climb
    on you or the bike   not breaking my legs.

In this smoke pink faux fur
        I space out my days   I slush through the cemetery
    on Christmas Eve   in my candle dress smoking
        in my crown of wet candles.
        I shush your therapy
missing the hot springs   and Edward G. Robinson.
          You say I get three dresses
      and the smell of couch/crotch
        and the smell of Christmas
    shiny red lips and scotch
in the parlor where we seem like   unethical diamonds
    bigger than horseflies.

In the pallor we seem to be entering   an era of surface.
        It's like roots or mildew
how all of the sudden I notice.

MADCAP / CHAMPAGNE HOURS

say little pity   my Hollyrot heart
      in a face freeze and solidity
the excuse cage kittening
      giving head in a dark movie set stairwell
and this might not be the right way
      and your message is death
and the duty is sleep   and suicidal ideation
      and no politics please
ballerina dresses   and fudge and a poodle skirt
      and we won't even listen   to cowboy noir on the radio.

      I try to catch up   I try not to freeze
the big cat's mouth looks   the same as a baby
            I hold the skull in my white chiffon
      and we can stuff the toy bear
with rotting fruit   then it explodes.
      I touched myself up there
            tried to feel I was pregnant
the pink palace is gone   the styrofoam heart
      conjures me eerily
            and I want to get higher   on your uncanny
yet I'm dead and black-lipped
            and the worms nurse my skeleton breasts
and I want to live in the middle of language
      and I want to live in a brain-shaped swimming pool
with all the dolls shaped like me
      drowning and dreaming and bouncing around.

MADCAP / BIG SKULL

Glittery foam hearts I don't understand
      pewter therapy   I don't wash my hands.
I've come a long way
      I touch my coarse cunt
the milk-and-pink stole swings below like a pendulum
      a long way of uncaring,   of honey, of caving.
The red berries on the tree means it's going to die
      day dreams of becoming a scarecrow
or fucking a scarecrow
      touching myself   I knew in advance
daydreams horror seeks   nothing to bring in
      except my sailor blouse   ripped at the breast
my stretchmarks   purple velvet
      how she said in the dressing room
did you get burned?   nothing to bring
      except drenched afternoons
drugged out in March
      watching Liz Taylor films in the day
Butterfield 8   Maggie the cat
      how March has big feet
idiosyncratic   how he busted in
      on my blonde/confiscating my pills
how you sent him to take all my pills.
      Every blonde dies in a carwreck
or at least loses her face
      and it's a thinkpiece to drink
my blood   or her blood
      but we never talk of it.

MADCAP /
SMOKY PINK SNAKE PIT INTROSPECTION

Make it stop on the one hand
        how a topcoat smooths everything
how you're tired on the other
        how the day after Christmas
you got snowed in at Kmart   with plaid shaving kilts
        with a man who kept saying his bloodtype
how you drank bourbon from a snack bar cup
        comfy-cozy in the baby department.
Make it stop on the one hand   how the blood man
        said you were a secret
your hair the color of his blue Christmas tree
        how you became profane instead of a baby
diamond on velvet   less sweet-faced, more angular
        how you walk across a graveyard
over and over   and sleep long hours
        wake up with a sore throat
and how you never went to your grandfather's grave.

The town made for peace has red trails through the woods
        where men wear hooves on their hands
where they never stop acting The Snow Queen.
        In the dream I was threatened
and overthrown   so I breastfed the mice
        but one mouse wanted jelly
and this town would never have a hut
        with a Tarot card reader

but the square and its lights grow on me
        needle shower, the keys
and so many things screenprinted
        and a New Year's Eve velvet jacket
embroidered with clocks   quantity/quality
            and new lives with beads
and so many things I can't take advantage of
        and so many men with braids and sweater vests
outside the bar.

I must have been brutal in Boston
        east of the sun. We murdered the man
who kept us apart
        so we can't stand each other
now I want to be picturesque
        icicles so long
they kill you or me
        and I hum to the underworld
try on all the fur coats
        in the thrift store in Kiev.

MADCAP / HOUSE OF MANSFIELD

I want to preserve   this room in rose
     so I can think in the heart house   but I never think
because what can you do
     when all you want is a snow-walk
in the middle of Hollyrot   but you sit on a swing
     with a daisy chain   try daily to exit your ego.
          I suppose they would call if you died
but I keep dreaming you die
     days without knowing
no response to the bones or the love poems.
          I drive my pink car
right into language is madness
     and dead lace transmissions.
     In my old age I get sloppy
in my old age I'm too late to the plays
     I write it out   once it's too much
my heart-shaped pool   my fairy-tale noose
     the red comes off easily
pretend newspapers and paper computers.
          You die in the house
built from strawberry girls and lemon-scent pencils and piss.
     You die in the attic
with a sun-catcher unicorn air-freshener.
     The 8-ball is right
I do need to concentrate
     and this is a party
in a cold alley   where your jiz could freeze

or this is a party   where I hide all the good booze
or this is a party of beauty.   I get all the steps
    and my breasts feed the world
with milk froth and fudge
    hearts in the snow
like I could be Mary
    and then the car wrecks
in my gory death   because I couldn't help it
    I married him since the oracle said
and my gory death
    chips my nails like a motherfucker.

STAR '80 PLANCHETTE

Exeunt mortality   personality   sentimentality
the little girl left   behind in her coffin
     no color left in her hair   candy floss
and the sheer   fact she was desultory
     posing naked while everyone moved.

Justice judging with difference, the draw
     or justice judging at Palm Springs atomic
with aqua blue radios   shining in eye walls
     or justice judging by freezing her body.

The unicorn is in memorium   the smell of a gunshot
     memorizing a horoscope
to be astral in hell.

You can live down a scandal if you want to
     you can work in a slaughterhouse
come out in a pink skirt and rollerskates
     sadness in your gut   Harlow's death like a gat
the set became quiet.

I don't want to foster your mourning
     horizon and the pressure   of bathing in a rain barrel
or a coffin   or a rotten   Venice Beach gondola.

You beg me to come fix   your degenerate landscape
        but you'd better eat the fish   while it still has a fever
you'd better swallow a lock of my hair
        you'd better get your nose butchered to look like me
outside melodrama
                and burning inside   the genie-shaped bottle
                the muscle contractions
        we used to call sex
                next to the bondage machine.

OLD HABITS / MADCAP OCELOT

This is a protectorate and I am the platinum
  petal-pusher and drinking
marks my hair rot and nails breaking
  and I will feel glam
ere I get kidney sick.
  I tried to watch the tell-all
to no avail its scratchy radio plot
  but knock me over with a pinecone
since I never get off. I never take off
the red velvet cape since I have no
  work ethic, get high
on blonde dye since I want to nestle
  in that special murky place
where they make scotch.
    There is something to this decade
sick of grey, smooth it down
  besides making movies but it doesn't matter
and I fuck too much symphony with my raspberry manicure
  beat drop and raspy disease.
My skin, my-stay-young-peel-off start disaster
  if I stay inside with your life of winter
my search for martinis romanticized.

  A kitten flick of the eye resuscitates
my starvation reincarnate
  no food, booze, and popcorn
I buy mink stoles that match the sick cold

as it gets easier to fuck
    in a world without love
my old habits   dyed black and solid
    and I will not star in a graveyard
unless that graveyard is Hollywood
    and I will line up my missed calls
my state-shaped necklaces
    my nails are a wreck
on your death anniversary
    thanks to Lana Turner and the bar in his car.
We should have chopped Lana's legs off
    and mopped up her green blood
with our furs.

MADCAP / STATION TO STATION

It's amazing how the future keeps leaving dark spots
        between dark melting snows and radio shows
depressive hedonia   what a mink does for justice.
        I take too many pills   I search all the frequencies
for Ray Sinatra's moonlight rhythms   the perfect nude nail
            but it's only Tuesday.
It's the southern room   with the Dracula scrapbook
        the blue typewriter crack   the kill-heavy lamp
the frost on the windows   the bump of cocaine
        the ghost leaves a cigar   a computerized call
    too foggy and sloppy   outside to walk.
What do I catch   in the crystal topcoat
    the antique wallpaper   a mysterious car in the lot
                and between the red pages
        Harlow's face in the heart mirror.
                He said meld your own style
    and a real masterpiece   hides jokes inside
        and he's dead now so what do I watch?
    I'm a soft vamp   brown cat eye
cheap lashes   my deerhead's made   of glittery plastic
    I lie in bed like a cross   try to breathe
        the mice have no eyes   and I cannot read
    all around me the ides   new moon and the dripping
        is it movement or atmosphere
is it gold high heels   always the finger
        lost first inside me
those tight dark days

and what films will time save?
I wear heart-shaped jewelry   eyes swing back and forth
        I have no empathy
a closet of old coats   enormous chess boards
        and through the window, the garage
the rhododendron melodrama   the complex space problems
        a kitten flick   a resuscitation.
I put on a full face of makeup alone
            and if you don't want to know
if your marriage is hollow, don't love or low.
        The beauty advice sticks in my head
but content kills kids   no reincarnation
            so I plan my own death
        the smoke pink faux fur
            doing wonders for my girlish morale.

MADCAP / BABYLIGHTS

Beauticians always talk about my end
      and I'll never wear another kind of bracelet again
and my roots are so dirty
and it's hard to be Jayne when Jean was so pure
      in white fur exchanging hearts and loops
with Eleanor Roosevelt.
      It's hard to be nothing but personality
you ask for sex and I hang up this phone
      I break off your horns.

Multiple pursuits make me sleepy
                  there's this whole pink universe I hate
where people fawn over fairy tales   I don't want to engage
but I'll wear all the shoes   with big hearts on them
      and kill all the men silently
                  with a powder puff scepter
      blue and gold makeup   a sick kind of break.

I want to be me again and walk under
      that glowing red watertank but time is so weird.
Everyone believes in their horoscopes
      and I shit out my pink toys over towers
I surmise and surround   myself with my stuffed lambs
      covered in dust.

Shake gently, apply color and wait. It's fevered and spooky
      but who hasn't jumped on her train?
      Criticism shifty-eyed in an alien language
where we meet for cold picnics   in a liminal cage
where I've grown antlers   and Harlow rabbit ears.

I'll make some money   and it will be ok
      but the dappled piglet will die.
It's staying light later
      but they're skiing hills bare
and the grass bleeds underneath
    and would the world be different for anyone
had I never engaged?
      I just pace in circles   in high-heels low-lit
beauticians tsk-tsking my roots.

MADCAP / KITTEN FLICK

Little deer on the last day
that's what gift giving is
        and I call this laziness
but it might be complexity
        plaid pants and black candles
the library non-light   that fills me with dread.

    In Georgia I kneel for forgiveness
in front of the Civil War wallpaper
        or drag a red bone across clay
    think fake swans are people on the brown lake
since we let her rot in a dark house last winter

        or suffer in pink smoke and faux fur
and peppermint   or say I'll eat later.
        I lucid dream six kids in snowpants
on the roof by the ocean in Boston or Russia.
        I don't own noir
and I have no strategy.   I weep at meat
        since everything I know
is an incoming pony corpse
        and the sleigh in the town square
is covered in blood.

The deaf boy from the movie
is painting our graves
        as I leave my mark in the dead mice
the fox light   the lip pulp   paper crowns
        lemon-scented pencils.
Every woman has a history of diaries
        mine are nothing special
every woman has a velvet momentum
        and I desire this scotch-drunk
sparkle forever   this blue bottlebrush tree
        this femme fatale   blue in her bodysuit
this cold curve of her ass.

MADCAP / THE FABULOUS CENTURY

In a way I'm the best sister
I keep vacillating between
        virgin and archer   booze and machine
buff blue   nail varnish and nest.

In this decade of fear   atomic transition
I masturbate with a brush
            in this decadence
I wish for Hawaii   thick skin on my legs
        power dissipates.
                    Push-push and an even
        harmonic heroic   I lie to myself and I'm lazy
I wake up to legal pads   when the boy just wants peace.
        I smash glasses on ships.
He says the worms die outside the body
        and it will forever precipitate
but no one will find out my secret.

        Take off your glasses. Draw wings or dashes.
It's hunger. I'm calling it action
        how I don't want to live like the others
bleeding cherry pastries and sucking off ghosts
        master/slave narrations   sad limitations.
I'll wear my smoke pink   faux fur and pretend
        I know something about fucking
and nuclear messes   look forward to radio transmission
        finding my purpose   a fast-drying topcoat

but purpose is shitty   and the clotheshorse is sick
    and I saw your unsafe mauve eyes
your radio play   the devil facing forward
    my drug under thrust.

You can tell imperfections
    when light's shining through.
I'm slick with death
    and baby I jangle
I slide my silk head
    right in your modern mouth.

MADCAP / DEPRESSIVE HEDONIA

How was it only an hour
  haunted dolls said *it's a holiday*
leave your keys on the desk and act harder
    put on your neon lace nightie
and lie in the spa tub to wait for the ghost
  rockabye/rockaway rip your fingernails off.

It's a zero sum game a time of amethyst
  last night I slept next to the man with black horns
I held the rod he held the needle
   a long line of pin-ups
   howled *evil eye.*
It takes so long to find the right trail
  so I walk across traffic electricity's wrong
   the egg-bread swan song
  my ass in houndstooth all my crises winking
capitalism ruins everything *but I love to buy shit*
   and I cannot remember California
  wood-painted silver old-fashioned handwriting.
   I cry by the graveyard
stopping to piss and every shopping center's bland
  even with Harlow fingernails
   and black leopard print
  a show-woman's glamor peppermint handoil
ceramic deer shakers a handful of pills.

I outline my thin lips in ink
I could hide here all night/not eat any dinner
remembering the blue paper rotating Christmas tree
how every year I sat   whining beside it.

Two girls walk by me   in whipped cream and cat ears.
I ask   *did you drink   some of my bone booze*
to turn yourselves into snow queens?

MADCAP ONE

I've seen enough of the vapors   I'm ready to scream in the lake
    okay by my coarse dress   okay by my lies
so many razors   some better than others
    lavender platinum   and soft hogs so thick
to touch up my manicure   you hate my solitude
      and it hasn't rained in a month.
I roll myself in faux fur   across the false crystal mine.
      What pigs did I even   try to say bye to?
Will I cry for the veins?
Will I cry for the vapors?
      The park ranger left his bad taste in my mouth.

      Nails and tails   look better done
but hell I don't bother   to wash my face.
      Draw me a bath   I'm not socratic. I'm not worth
dressing up for. I look best as a pink ham
    draw me a bath   in the sassafras dressing room
not as elaborate. Give me a tax break.

      I'll don your toga   I'll nap in my decoupaged coffin
psychotic on Templeton whiskey   I'll fuck in any language.
    Draw me a false bath   on the wrong map
      draw me a diamond.
    There are crystals inside me and balls   but the hall of rocks
closed like it did in the 70s

and I'm comfortable with the limits of my history
and my suicide   is its own excuse
and I'll leave you my best liquors   not the guest soup.

MADCAP / DEADSTOCK
(THE GIRL CAN'T HELP IT)

What does it mean   not settling down
      your sex or deathtrap
to satin trouble in paradise?
    What does it mean when you look at the clock
decide to focus in winter
     on styrofoam hearts
     a purity war-torn
a Cupid box wrapped   in white butcher paper
     and refuse to be flattered?

    I don't know what I should do besides faint
the candles are hard   dollheads dovetail
    from the ceiling.
    I desperately write all the songs
what I know best is hunger
    unwashed pillowslip hair and orange lipstick
how with plastic crystals
    they blame women for everything.

    I waited for you   macabre Valentine
my bloody story   in retrospect
    I painted my nails like hooves every day
a guillotine virgin   a subliterate physical myth
    from the heart my dark drugs
my tartan hairbow   my sweetheart bracelet
    monogrammed   *Red + Chet*

etched with fangs   the brass deer on the table
     the northern lights trapped in a fishtank.

I suckle pale pink.   I'm sick of pale pink.
     I'm wet and I wear   my lace harness on stage
breasts even bigger   on my broadening ribcage.
     Cross your fingers my husband
gets killed at the end of the movie
     as we dream and release.
Cross your fingers this heart-shaped
     horsepill lets us sleep.

MANSFIELD / MADCAP / POCONOS

My new shtick will be aging
and envy   but it should be forgiveness
    letting out breaths
but it will be wet leaves and Hollyrot.
    I don't care about your witchcraft
    but I wear a scarab   I care not about armories
plastic carnival pearls
    and I wear oxblood oxfords at the campground armada.
      I will shatter the Predicta
    I'll slash our wrists. I don't care in the mud
if this is still winter   hunting or fishing
    you have your sob story
I have my dark roots.
                  I climb the tree
    that says do not resuscitate
rip out the country song hair
    stick a broom in my crotch
stick a candle in the empty gin bottle
    and let me put it this way
your sapphire horoscopes are nothing
    and that's not my crying
that's rain on the window
    and let's roll the dead deer in glitter
climb through the cracked glass
    to the heart-shaped hottub
in the left-for-dead honeymoon suite.

MADCAP / WINTRY MIX

I don't need more horror   dry to the touch.
        I move in the cold
                and I lack mythology.
I watch conspirators   in windowpane glasses
            and herringbone tweed
long for beauticians   decapitation, Biloxi
        and steamy hot drug days
        dry radio plays.

I watch the time   like a soap opera
        the same paisley dress
black hair and frost.
            This false house is painful
        as you claim   the six love words I'll swallow
addicted to hearts and loop earrings
                or crimping or cramping
            addicted to porn or the phone
                or not being too young
and do women with red fingernails
        have red toes when socks are too thick to see?

I peel off the label   saying it's you
            all the skulls lining
        the path to the hothouse.
I consult meaty horoscopes
        I'm consulting my dreams
alone in fur boots   I have big disease.

I'm naked drinking scotch in the pasture
too many cymbals
or I'm waking up naked
stuck in an ice-skating movie.

MADCAP

ACKNOWLEDGMENTS

Thank you to the editors of these publications in which many poems from MADCAP first appeared, sometimes in earlier versions:

Blue Fifth Review, Otoliths, Uppagus, Sporklet, Mannequin Haus, taxicab magazine, where is the river :: a poetry experiment, Glass: A Journal of Poetry, SCAB, Spider Mirror Journal, FLAPPERHOUSE, Vagabond City, Bad Pony, Pom Pom, Waxing & Waning, GASHER, Sad Girl Review, The Hunger, glitterMOB, South Broadway Ghost Society, Redheaded Stepchild, MUSH/MUM, and Bone Bouquet.

Many of these poems were written during my artist residencies at the Kimmel Harding Nelson Center for the Arts in Nebraska City, NE; at Hot Springs National Park, Hot Springs, AR; and at Newnan ArtRez in Newnan, GA. I am very grateful to these organizations for providing me time and space to create.

"Madcap/Touch Up": The phrase that Jean Harlow made "too many films with titles like Bombshell" comes from the book Movie Star: A Look at the Women Who Made Hollywood by Ethan Mordden.

"House of Wax/Good Scotch for Pain": The phrase "Lombard was an absurdist" comes from the book Movie

Star: A Look at the Women Who Made Hollywood by Ethan Mordden.

"Bathhouse of Wax/Madcap Comes Across": "Since comedy is a long-shot/I don't need the tragedy face" is a play on the Buster Keaton quotation at the beginning of this book.

"Live to Tell" is a 1986 song by Madonna.

"You Wreck Me" is a 1995 song by Tom Petty.

"Did She Go to Hell? Yes, and They Called It Hollywood" is a photo caption in the book *Movie Star: A Look at the Women Who Made Hollywood* by Ethan Mordden.

Sparkle Plenty is a character in the Dick Tracy comics.

Star '80 is the title of a 1983 film about the life and death of Dorothy Stratten.

Our Dancing Daughters is the title of a 1928 film.

Strange Interlude is the title of a 1928 play by Eugene O'Neill and a 1932 film based on the play.

"Take Me Naked if It Makes Me Real Again": The phrase "no frigate like a book" is from poem #1286 by Emily Dickinson.

Station to Station is a 1976 album by David Bowie.

The Girl Can't Help It is a 1956 film starring Jayne Mansfield.

Jessie Janeshek is the author of *The Shaky Phase* (Stalking Horse Press, 2017) and *Invisible Mink* (Iris Press, 2010). Her chapbooks include *Spanish Donkey/Pear of Anguish* (Grey Book Press, 2016), *Rah-Rah Nostalgia* (dancing girl press, 2016), *Supernoir* (Grey Book Press, 2017), *Auto-Harlow* (Shirt Pocket Press, 2018), *Hardscape* (Reality Beach, forthcoming), and *Channel U* (Grey Book Press, forthcoming). She co-edited *Outscape: Writings on Fences and Frontiers* (KWG Press, 2008). She holds a Ph.D. from the University of Tennessee-Knoxville and an M.F.A. from Emerson College.

jessiejaneshek.net.